When One Door Closes

Wisdom From The East

To Find Your Soul's Path

Written By

Kaz Iso

Dedication

This book is dedicated to every individual who would like to know how to find your soul's path.

Table of Contents

Read This First

In this book, I talk about the benefit of Zen. You'll get the most value from the book if you download and use this **FREE** Zen Training Kit.

TO DOWNLOAD, GO TO
www.kaziso.com/freezenkit

Introduction

Have you ever felt like your path is closing in on you, or that nothing seems to be going your way? Sometimes it may feel like obstacles are being thrown at you, left and right. What if these challenges were actually gifts from the Universe to help you turn your life around? What if they were a suggestion from up above to change lanes in your life?

In Japan, there is a saying: "When God closes a door in your life path, God also opens a door for you."

What this is saying is that when a door is closing, there is ALWAYS a door opening as well.

When things seem to be against you, it is often a nudge from the Universe to change something in your life. Perhaps it is changing a job, or leaving a relationship, or relocating, or just shifting what you have been doing.

Why does this happen? The answer is simple. It is because we are all supposed to find happiness in our lives. Let me repeat that once again. **We are all supposed to find happiness in our lives.** I know this is a bold statement, but I am serious about this.

Through decades of life coaching, and having seen thousands transformed in Japan, my lifework and mission, is to educate the entire world about this great truth of life.

This book is dedicated to explaining how the universe works to support you, and how you can find happiness, no matter where you are in life.

When a door closes, there is always another door opening. Often the path you find after moving beyond your challenges is your soul's path.

So, how do you find that open door? How do you find your soul's path?

This book is written precisely to answer that question. It explains how to find your soul's path, one step at a time.

The concepts in this book may be new to some. The key is to remain open. Do not hate or dismiss ideas simply because you are not familiar with them. The guidance in this book may create new perspectives on your life, and considering new perspectives never hurts, especially those that have transformed millions of lives in the East.

So, here we go. Let us begin the journey to find your soul's path.

Kaz Iso

Chapter One

How to Find an Open Door

We've all heard the saying, "When one door closes, another door opens." Every time I am confronted with a challenge, I immediately look for the open door. I know there is always a new opportunity being presented to me just around the corner. I want you to know that is true in your life, too. Whether the issue is about work, relationship, or family, when one door closes, another always opens. The universe is constantly showing you the path with the most spiritual growth that will ultimately lead you to happiness.

You are a soul. Period. Trying to understand your life without recognizing the soul is like trying to explain life on earth without acknowledging the impact of solar energy. They are both invisible, but the effects are undeniable.

Your soul knows all the answers for your life. It knows where you came from, and it knows which path will bring you the greatest joy. We all have a life navigation system inside of us. All you have to do is learn how to access it.

We are here for spiritual growth so there are absolutely no coincidences in life. Everything that happens in life is meant to serve your transformation, but you have to choose it. You can accept that and find growth or deny it and be the passive recipient of life events—or worse, take on a victim mindset.

Existence becomes fulfilling when you find your soul's path. There is a purpose to everything we experience, and when you are open to this concept, a whole new perspective arises within you.

In my definition, feelings are messages from your soul while emotions are not. If you follow your feelings, or guidance from your soul, it will help you navigate to where you want to be in life, whereas emotions will not. If you believe you have been following your feelings and are not getting closer to where you want to be, you may have been unknowingly following your emotions instead.

Often the go-ahead message you receive from your soul is a feeling of quiet excitement. Extreme excitement tends to come from your emotions. It is therefore critical that you know the difference between the two because they often take you to two different destinations. To figure out the difference, you can start by paying close attention to what is going on in your mind and observe the results of your actions. The results will tell you whether you are listening to your feelings or your emotions.

Are you ready for this journey? If so, the best place to start is learning how to quiet your mind. It does not matter whether you call it Zen or meditation. It is not a religious ritual. It is a practical way to listen to your soul, one that has been utilized in the East for centuries. We'll get into the details of how to do this shortly.

The Impact of Real Life Examples

In each chapter I will relate a story of how one of my clients initially felt stuck behind a closed door but learned to find an open one.

Example #1: Hana's Story

I worked with a fascinating woman named Hana who was a really great Aura Soma reader. Aura Soma is a holistic therapy in which visual and non-visual vibrations of color, crystals, and aromas combine with light to harmonize the body, mind and soul. She used Aura Soma bottles to tell people what was going on in their mind. She was certified and was the second highest income generator for that particular Aura Soma association in Japan. However, one of the executives from the Aura Soma association told her to stop what she was doing because she was going beyond what she was taught. She was intuitive, or psychic, so she was giving her own advice in addition to the Aura Soma readings. The executive told her not to do anything extra, to just stay with her training. This discouraged her, and she didn't want to continue her work with that restriction.

She had been living in the western part of Japan, so she decided to try something different. She moved to Tokyo and got a job as a line assembly employee at a manufacturing factory, a big change for her. That position stressed her out so much that she became depressed, her skin broke out, and she started to show signs of other physical symptoms. That's when she came to my retreat in Sedona, AZ. In Sedona and during our private sessions, I told her that she was very talented. I suggested that just because one person told her something she didn't like did not mean she needed to quit what she was doing. I also told her that she could always find a creative way to do a job that serves other people.

With the power of Sedona and with a little bit of advice from me, she became motivated and empowered. She made the decision to leave the job that depleted her energy and instead pursue her dream. Once she made that decision, interesting things started to happen. She started to release a lot from her body, and every time this happened, she felt lighter and lighter. What was happening with her? When you let go of bad thoughts, your body starts to let go of all the negativity you bottled up while stressed. It was a sure sign that she was moving in the right direction.

So, what happened after Sedona? She left the factory job and started her own business. Now she is thriving, and many people, including my clients, love her unique Aura Soma sessions. In fact, she gave me a reading too, and it was incredible. All of this happened when she simply decided to follow her own path to happiness.

When she worked at the factory, she felt like the door was closing on her so she decided to get help in finding her happiness. Her soul spoke to her, but initially she did not know how to listen to it. When she learned how to listen to her Life GPS, she intuitively realized her calling. Then everything started to come into place for her and today she is an incredible intuitive reader.

Chapter Two

How to Connect with Your Inner Self

Almost all self-help books or spiritual leaders talk about having a relationship with your inner self. This relationship is important because unless you have a healthy relationship with your inner self, you can't have healthy relationships with others. A relationship with one's inner self can be vocal or non-vocal. In many cases, non-vocal communication is more important than vocal communication. Most people don't speak out loud to communicate with their inner selves. The conversation with your inner self happens quietly inside your mind. Just because you can't hear it doesn't mean communication isn't happening. In fact, it is happening constantly. For example, let's say you make a mistake and feel you can't live up to your own expectations. In your mind, you might say something like, "I'm the worst. I messed up again. I keep making the same mistakes over and over." We all have these silent communications with our inner self.

Your thoughts come from your active mind, whereas your feelings come from your inner self, your soul. So when you have a big decision you need to make in your life, you have two basic approaches you can take to find an answer. You could ask yourself, "What do I think about this?" Or you could ask yourself, "How do I feel about this?" These two questions will produce very different results. When you ask the question, "What do I think?" you come up with intelligent, logical answers based on analysis. On the other hand, when you ask yourself, "How do I feel?" you come up with feelings, which are answers that come to you directly from the source. To get the feeling answer, you must listen deeply to know what you want in your soul. This is the direction you want to follow.

Does this mean that we shouldn't ask ourselves what we think? Of course not. When making decisions, whether large or small, you need to know both how you feel and what you think. The important thing is to know which answer you have received – did you receive the feeling answer or the thought answer? The feeling answer will show you what to do, and the thought answer will often show you how to do it. However, try not to let your thought answer change your direction. I recommend asking your feeling question first so that you can receive your feeling answer without the influence of the mind.

Communication with your inner self is vital. When faced with a decision, people sometimes get several opinions, weigh each one, and make decisions aimed at pleasing someone else. How many of you chose a career because it pleased your family? Many people feel compelled to please others instead of pleasing their inner selves. Other people make a choice because that's what "everybody" says is best, even when they do not necessarily agree. Most people do not spend enough time communicating with their inner selves. By making decisions based on outside influences, it is much less likely you will move in the soul's direction. I'm not saying never to ask others for guidance. What I'm saying is that listening to your inner self will help you make the decision that serves you the best. It's imperative that the decision you are making is pleasing to your inner self, or your soul, not to anybody else. Do your best not to allow another persons' energy or influence to change the course of your decision.

When you keep making choices and decisions based on the external influences around you without spending time with your inner self, it won't be long until you lose track of who you are. Every decision has an impact on your life. Let's say you decide to do something that you are not 100% happy about. Your fake self-image will be presented to the outside world and you will be out of sync because what you are feeling at the soul-level does not match what you are living on the outside. When you pretend you're somebody else for a long time, you take on a different persona. Then there is an expectation for you to make similar decisions, and as that gains momentum, you move further and further away from who you really are. You can see how easy it is to lose track of yourself when you are not in touch with your inner self.

This was the case with a woman you will hear about in Chapter 6 who was struggling with her business, trying to get rid of inventory. When she simply trusted the message from her soul, her business turned around in a dramatic way. Know that the message from your soul is always right, and if you listen to it, good things will always happen. Remember that feelings are guidance from the Universe. If you know what you're feeling and what you're thinking, and you know the difference between the two, that's the greatest wisdom you can have.

The law of the Universe is absolute and it works with everyone. You are not the exception. Believe that when there is a closing door, there is also an open door. Listening is the first step. If you truly believe what you hear from your soul, that belief will help you find an open door. Ask yourself, where is the open door? What am I happy doing? What is pulling me? A lot of people are deep thinkers, but the goal is to listen to that feeling coming from within.

All the steps I talked about rely on the ability to listen to your inner self and your Life GPS. That will make a huge difference in your life.

Example #2: Miho's Story
A woman named Miho was in her thirties when she first came to my workshop. Miho was unhappy and depressed. She was not happy with herself and felt unworthy. She was not happy with her son either.

When she came to my workshop she told me that she had some problems with her son. But it wasn't her son that had the problem; it was her belief system and expectations that were perpetuating a scarcity mentality. This scarcity mindset was instilled by her parents. She was stuck in a cycle of, "I am not enough," and "I do not have enough." We talked and discovered different ways she could think. First, she had been thinking that things needed to be exactly the way she expected, and when they weren't, she considered herself a failure. She learned to let go of this belief, which in turn, relieved the tension with her son.

She also began to understand the concept of the scarcity mentality that she had been living with. When she came to understand the importance of self-love and acceptance, her face brightened noticeably.

It took a couple sessions at my workshops for her to truly understand the concept and integrate it on an emotional level but once she did, her mindset shifted and changed completely. It's one thing to understand the concept logically; it's quite another thing to internalize it and create a new belief.

After her mindset shifted, she found a job that she loved as a spiritual travel advisor and agent. She started running spiritual tours in Japan. Then she met her soul mate. With both her personal life and her career on track, her happiness emerged.

Initially, she was in a place where she was not happy about herself or her son, and was unsure what to do with her life. This was a sign from the Universe to change from the inside. What needed to change was not her son but her mindset; once she did that, everything smoothed out. So, when the Universe closed one door, it opened another, revealing her true happiness, a fulfilling career, and a loving relationship with her soul mate.

Chapter Three

How to Activate Your Life GPS

Your Life GPS is the part of you that has deep wisdom about what is best for your life. You could also call it your higher self or your inner self. The terminology isn't as important as understanding the concept. You have a system inside of you that knows which path will make you happy and which will provide the most spiritual growth. The way to hear the messages from your GPS is by calming your mind.

Imagine rough ocean water during a hurricane with big waves rolling on the water. Most people would be smart enough to stay away from the water during this time. Well, a while back, I was into scuba diving and a colleague and I were on vacation when a hurricane was rolling in. Despite the warnings, we decided to go diving, which was a big mistake. Luckily, we survived! However, even though the surface water was very rough, it was a lot quieter just a bit further down.

Your mind is like that. On the surface, there are a lot of things going on. Your mind is always busy thinking of something. Data shows that about 50,000-70,000 thoughts come across your mind each day. By quieting your mind, you can access your Life GPS. Or to put it another way, when your mind is less busy, you are better able to hear the subtle messages coming from your Life GPS. Your Life GPS is always there and is always active. It's the communication path that needs to be cleared, activated, or strengthened by quieting the chatter in your mind. So, how do you listen to the messages from your Life GPS?

Step 1 is to believe that Life GPS exists. When you doubt, it creates a doubtful frequency, and nothing comes to fruition. When you believe, you have a far better chance of getting messages from your Life GPS.

In Step 2, you must believe that you have the ability to receive all of the

9

information. If you haven't done it before, you can't be sure that you will be able to do it. But when you believe you can achieve something, it's 100 times easier to be successful. So it is helpful to believe that you can receive the information.

Step 3 is preparing your question. It's good to prepare a question before you delve into your mind. Write it down or commit it to memory. However, make sure you only have one question to ask so that it is easy to remember and you can focus on it.

In Step 4, when the environment is calm, begin practicing Zen. I use the term Zen because that's what I learned in Japan, but some people call it meditation and that's perfectly fine.

Start by sitting in a comfortable position. If you sit in a chair, do not cross your legs, as that will hinder your energy from flowing smoothly. You could also sit on the floor in any style that's comfortable for you. Just remember to keep your spine straight. It's best to do this when you are not disturbed by any outside media, friends or family. Disconnect from everything in your environment.

Close your eyes and breathe out slowly. Simply focus on exhaling as slowly as possible. Start with 10 seconds, and if it's comfortable, increase to 15 or 20 seconds. When you focus on exhaling, you breathe in naturally. When you engage in slow, deep breathing, your brainwaves will start to change. People are often in the Beta state, an active mind state, but when you start breathing slower, the brain goes into the Alpha state, a state of relaxing, like when taking a bath.

Through training, you may learn to enter a deeper state of mind called the Theta state, which is like the borderline between sleep and awake. In this state, your consciousness is very clear but your body is almost asleep. It's hard to know when you have achieved the Theta state for the first time because when you think too much, your mind will go back to Alpha or Beta state. When you have achieved the Theta state, or you feel more relaxed than ever before, move on to Step 5. If you do not achieve the Theta state in the beginning, however, that's perfectly ok. You can also do this from the Alpha state, which is even easier.

Step 5 is to ask your question. When you ask a question, whatever pops up in your mind first is the answer from your Life GPS.

Step 6 is recognizing what pops up in your mind. Sometimes you receive the answer in the form of words; other times it will manifest in the form of feelings. Let's say the question you ask is: "Should I stay at this job or get a new one?" If the feeling that you receive is "I've had enough" or if you don't feel comfortable when you think about staying in that work environment, then your Life GPS is telling you to move on.

Sometimes an image will pop into your head. For example, let's say the question that you asked your Life GPS is "What do I want to do?" If you receive an image of yourself walking in the mountains, then just go hiking. You might doubt that going out hiking will resolve your issue or help you find what you want to do in your life. However, when you go hiking, you will receive all of Nature's power. This will put you in a good mental and physical state. You will be alone, completely surrounded by nature, away from electromagnetic fields, and have plenty of time to think. It will also afford you time to stop thinking, which will put you in the perfect state to receive the inspiration you've been looking for.

Another way some people receive guidance from their Life GPS is by hearing a voice. Some people hear a voice that sounds like it's coming from behind them, or some people hear their own voice quietly in their mind. Normally when you hear a voice, it's a very simple sentence such as 'go' or 'talk' or 'good.' When you hear a voice saying something rather complicated, such as, "If you go that way, then you must do this and that," it's your mind instead of a message from your Life GPS. A message from higher wisdom is always simple.

Some people see visions with feelings. Let's say you'd like to know what career to pursue and you are excited by a vision of yourself speaking on stage. You might realize that instead of finding a new job, you are meant to start your own business and become a speaker. Although, just by seeing this vision, you may not know what your next step should be. So, repeat the same process and ask, "What do I do next?" If you see yourself reading a book, the next step might be to go to a bookstore or library and get a book.

There are also some people who go into a deeper state and experience a sense of knowing. I get a sense of knowing more often than seeing or hearing. For example, the question might be, "Should I stay in this relationship or move on?" By going into the deeper state of mind, they have that knowing that the relationship is not serving them and that things will work out fine after leaving the relationship.

Your Life GPS can also send messages by a sensation running through your body. For example, let's say you'd like to know if you should move forward with a joint venture but you have concerns in your conscious mind, so you decide to ask your Life GPS what to do. You prepare your question, quiet your mind, and go into a deeper state. When you ask the question, your mind is quiet. When you imagine yourself participating in the joint venture, the sensation of excitement runs through your body. That's an instant message from the Universe, or from your Life GPS, telling you that is the way to go.

It's important to keep in mind that when you experience an electric sensation when your mind is active, it might not be coming from your Life GPS. Instead, it might be your imagination thinking about getting a lot of money. That is an emotion, not a feeling. It's a subtle difference and it takes practice and experience to tell the difference. But when you are in the deeper state and you receive a message from deep within, you will be able to tell it is a message from Life GPS, not from your emotional, conscious mind.

To receive a message from your Life GPS, just be open. You may receive your message in a way that's different from anything I have described. So be open and aware that any subtle feeling might be an answer from your Life GPS. Remember, you almost never receive information with a huge drum roll introduction and dramatic voice declaring, "Here is the way to go." Unfortunately, it doesn't work like that. Do not beat yourself up or keep thinking, "Why am I not receiving a message?" When you stop doubting, that's when you allow the information to come to you.

Also, instead of trying to go and get the answer, allow the information to come to you. A lot of people need to get out of their own way to receive a message. When your mind and body are stiff, you cannot relax. That is not a state in which you can receive a message. Just relax and let thoughts go as much as possible. You probably haven't gone through training like this during your education so it will take some practice. But with practice anyone can do it because the ability is built into your system--no mistake, no exceptions.

Step 7 is very simple, but not easy. It requires you to accept the message. A lot of people have difficulty with this. When they receive a message, many people turn on their conscious minds and start doubting. When you do not feel that you deserve success or have the ability to succeed, or you feel that you don't have sufficient resources to make something happen, you abandon the message.

Keep in mind that you will figure out "how" later. Do not let concern about the "how" change the guidance that you receive. This is very important. Just receive and trust it for now and figure out the rest later.

Do not start doubting. It's a good idea to write down the message exactly as you receive it so that you do not forget it or alter it in your memory.

To expand on this, let's consider an example. Let's say that your current job is not serving you well, and you feel like it's time for you to change lanes. So you sit and practice Zen. The message you receive is to leave your current job and start your own business. You do some research to figure out how to start your own business, and in that process, you realize how many things you would need to do to make it happen and you become overwhelmed. Fear then starts kicking in because you have never started a business before. Being overwhelmed and filled with fear, you decide to get a new job instead of starting your own business. This is a typical example of letting the "how" change what you do. If the message you receive is start your own business, stick with that. In this information age, "how" is actually not that difficult once you put your mind and time into it.

Just as important is to trust the information that you receive. You will figure out how to pull it off later, but first, trust that it is information from your Life GPS. Make a move with the message. It takes faith and courage but once you experience success, it will give you a whole new perspective on life.

What I have been describing is a process of accessing "Infinite Intelligence." Your personal knowledge is limited, but access to this intelligence is within you. So, you either live believing in what's visible, what has been proven by science, or you broaden your horizon a bit and live a life based on belief in that which has not yet been proven. I respect science, but at the same time, the Universe is far larger than what we have seen and proven. We observe the solar system and we know the Earth is spinning, but we cannot replicate these phenomena. There is greater intelligence that is making all of it possible.

The intelligence of the universe is far greater than our own, and what I am describing is a process to trust the Infinite Intelligence that's within you. Imagine there is a mailbox inside of your mind. You probably know that the mailbox outside your house is not going to receive a message from God. God is not going to use that mailbox so you need this mailbox inside your mind to receive a message from higher intelligence. It doesn't matter what you call it - yourself, higher self, inner self, or a spiritual guide. There are a lot of names to choose from. The purpose of this process is simply to receive a message from inside. If you receive a message and it helps make your life better, does it matter where it comes from?

A lot of religious people fight over what to call this higher intelligence. Spirituality allows you to simply believe what you believe, let other people believe what they believe, and be okay with the differences. Do not start a war. Do not start attacking people who think differently. So Step 7 is to receive and accept the message from your Life GPS without judging it or its source.

The 8th and final step is to activate this muscle regularly. Your Life GPS is always there. It is always available but you must engage the communication path to listen to its subtle messages. For example, when you do pushups every single day, you build muscle. Listening to your Life GPS messages works in a similar way. When you ask a question and receive the information, either by word, sensation, voice, or vision, you are building your inner muscle to receive messages. The more you do it, the better the muscle works. So simply repeat this process to become good at receiving messages.

Example #3: Tomoko's Story
This story is about a woman named Tomoko who didn't have the confidence to do energy healing. She was afraid of rejection because some people think of energy healing as witchcraft. So she decided to

become a physical therapist instead. Everything was fine until she started to feel that physical therapy was not what she wanted to do for the rest of her life. She felt the need to change lanes, so she came to my workshop and we talked. I told her that energy healing is great, and there are a lot of people in America doing it. There are people who believe in it and others who don't, and that's perfectly fine. She just needed to find the believers and let go of her fear of rejection. The actual conversation was a little longer, but this is what I said in a nutshell.

So, she decided to leave her old business and start her new business in energy work. Interestingly, without any aggressive advertising, customers came in droves by word of mouth and she made enough money in her first year to come to my retreat in Italy. She is very happy she made that change and she now teaches other healers to become certified. It all happened because she learned to listen to her life GPS and changed lanes when things were feeling off.

Chapter Four

The Power of Beliefs

In this chapter, we will talk about the power of beliefs. Throughout this book, we have discussed that when there is a door closing in your life, there is always an open door as well--you just have to find it. However, not everybody is able to do that successfully. Why? What makes the difference? Why can some people hear this and apply it immediately, whereas other people hear it but are not able to make the change? The difference is the power of belief.

Let's say something bad happens to you and as a result you become sad, angry, upset, etc. When that happens, you are not able to find an open door. So you need to be able to manage your emotions, and the way to do that is by shifting your focus and perspective. When you think that what happened is awful, then it becomes a horrible thing in your life; but when you decide to apply a positive spin to the event, it will create a new positive emotion. This spin is possible if you believe that when something "bad" happens, it is nothing but a nudge from the Universe to change lanes. It is simply an experience from which you can learn and grow.

This ability to shift your beliefs is not built in a day. I suggest not just reading this book once, but over and over until these lessons become a part of you. When you believe that what you read in this book is true, and you start looking at your life through that lens, you will find similar situations in your own life. When that happens, your belief will become stronger. Also, when you experience something "bad" and you are able to shift your mindset and turn it into a positive, then your belief in finding an open door will be much stronger. Experience can strengthen your beliefs. This is the key to making the switch from a closing lane to an open one.

I have a step-by-step formula to follow when bad things happen to you. You can always come back to this portion of the book and apply it.

Step 1: Establish a positive mindset. When something bad happens, people normally experience negative emotions, but to find an open door you must be in a positive frequency or mindset. An open door can't be found when you are in a victim mindset. So if something bad happens, and you are able to stay in a positive mindset, that's great. If your mindset is negative, then step one is to go from a negative zone to a positive zone in your emotional frequency. Do that by looking for the spiritual meaning to the event that has just occurred. You are here for the spiritual growth, so the question is, "If what happened is the best thing for my spiritual growth, how is this situation going to help me grow?" When you ask a question like that, you will surely be able to find an answer. Why? Because your soul has all the answers.

Here is an example. A client was being physically abused by her father, and at one point thought her life was ruined. She was miserable and did not feel good about herself or her life. She wanted to find a way to get away from her father, so she decided to spend a year as an exchange student in the United Stated. That year provided her a lot of new experiences and helped rid her of her victim mindset. She was exposed to many different perspectives on life, which gave her a new perspective on her own life. She went back to Japan as a much stronger person.

When she now looks back, she does not view the original situation as horrible and does not view herself as a victim. She likes who she became. She also knows that she wouldn't be where she currently is without experiencing everything she went through. Going to America had a life changing impact, and she knows she wouldn't have gone if her father hadn't abused her. She is now convinced that what happened was designed for her spiritual growth. Having found an open door when she was so stressed and weak, she now has confidence that she will be able to find an open door again when something challenging happens in her life.

We are all human. So in the moment when something bad happens, it's perfectly okay to experience negative emotions for a little while. It is helpful to remember, though, that there is always spiritual learning available from any situation, no matter how negative. If you hear this message for the first time when you are already in a negative situation and going through an emotional storm, it's harder to believe it. So the trick is to learn this lesson when your mind is positive and open.

Step 2: Be open to receiving guidance from the Universe in many different ways. I often see people expecting to receive a message in a certain way. For example, one person believes that he needs to hear the message to believe it is coming from within. Other people feel that they need to see a clear image, convinced that "seeing is believing." But there are literally hundreds of ways you could receive a message. Sometimes it's the first paragraph you see when you open a book, other times it could be what you see on television. So be open to receiving messages in different ways. Sometimes it shows up as inspiration, and other times it is just a phone call from a friend. Maybe you're talking with a friend about your college days and then one little word from them wakes you up, and you suddenly know what you need to do. Do not think that guidance from the Universe comes in only one way, because if you do, you might miss a critical message.

Here is one unique way I received guidance from the universe in a critical moment. A long time ago, I went to Niagara Falls with my parents. In the lobby of the hotel, my mom fell down and hit her lower jaw pretty hard and almost got a concussion. She turned pale and sickly and needed to rest. With the way she looked, I thought our fun was over because she'd probably have to stay in the hotel the rest of the trip. I wondered if I should just wait or if I should do something. As I was thinking about it, almost unconsciously, I turned on the television.

As soon as I turned on the TV, the guy on the screen said, "Don't take a chance." I felt that was a message from the Universe so I immediately decided to arrange for a remote healing for my mom.

At the time, I had experienced remote healing for myself, but I wasn't sure if remote healing could work for my mother's situation. I decided to try it anyway. I spoke with a healer and she said she would start the healing between 9:00 and 9:15pm. She told me to tell my mom to lie down, be quiet, and be open to and conscious of the healing energy that she would be receiving. Then, about a half hour later, since she was in the adjacent suite, I opened the door to see how she was doing. My mom was just walking around like nothing had happened, feeling completely fine. I asked what happened and she said, "It was a very interesting experience. I was lying down, and then started to feel some heat or energy around my head, and that started to go down. Then maybe 10 minutes later I started to feel just fine." The next day she was walking everywhere and we were able to resume our vacation, all because I received the words from the television as a message from the Universe.

Step 3: Keep your receiving antenna sensitive and keen. This is important because messages from the universe are always subtle. As I said earlier, there is no drum roll or mail in your mailbox. Some people hear a message loud and clear, but for most beginners, you barely hear anything. Or when you have your eyes closed and you see an image, the moment you think about it or doubt it, the image disappears. So whether it's listening, seeing or knowing, it's important to have your antenna open, sensitive, and keen.

Step 4: Once you receive the direction, act on it. This is probably the most important step of all. When people receive direction, many sit on it and don't do anything about it. They start doubting and drop it. Then nothing changes. Sometimes it's just a little thing that you need to do—maybe even one phone call, as in my case.

No matter what the message is, just receive it and act on it. When you've had one positive experience after following these four steps, this will strengthen your belief. When your belief is stronger and something challenging happens the next time, you will be able to go into the right mindset so that you can find an open door much more easily.

Belief is a choice. People have their belief systems instilled by their parents, teachers, or other seniors and these beliefs may require some undoing. I invite you to believe that no matter what happens in your life, you are not a failure and that when there is a closing door, you can always find an open one. These are very powerful beliefs to live with. They can only help you. I suggest trying out these beliefs, applying them to your life, and seeing what happens. Out of hundreds of thousands of clients with whom I've worked, I've never seen a failure. I've seen many people who doubted in the beginning, but once a little success occurred, then people believed and good things happened to them.

Belief is what determines your action and decisions. Everybody faces challenging situations. If you have the knowledge that you can find an open door when you encounter a tough situation, you will have no fear. When you have no fear, your mind is lighter and filled with happiness. To believe that you can always find an open door is a blessing.

I suggest that you read this book over and over, maybe for the next three to four weeks, until this becomes your belief. Then, when something bad happens, it will be almost impossible not to remember this concept that you have impressed into your mind. You will immediately recall that there is an open door available to you even in the worst of times.

Example #4: Masako's Story

A woman named Masako felt stuck in her marriage to a man from a traditional, conservative, and prestigious family. Her mother-in-law was vicious and only cared about the woman doing things her way. Somehow, she put up with that marriage for more than 30 years. She was depleted, but she stayed because she couldn't get over the fear of losing everything, especially her financial security. Then one day she started to find her answer through spirituality. She realized that she was not actually stuck, but had just believed she was. She realized that she had a choice. She was mostly making the choice to stay out of fear of financial instability. Nonetheless, the pain became so intense that she decided to make the change. She left her marriage, and even though her finances changed, she became a lot happier. Though her new apartment is a lot smaller than her previous residence, she learned that happiness is not in a house, but in her mind. This shift happened when she finally realized that she was not actually stuck in her marriage and that another door was open to her.

Chapter Five

The Power of Empty Mind

You can change your belief system if you are open to it. By open I mean that first, the lid of your mind needs to be open, so to speak. Second, you must be willing to change your particular mix of beliefs, whether they are positive or negative. Third, you must be willing to let go of a belief or belief system if it doesn't serve you.

A lot of people resist this, at least partly because they feel like they would be losing a part of themselves, but that's not the case. Imagine you are a circle. Whatever belief system you have, imagine that it is outside of you. When you let go of a belief, or change the mix of your beliefs, you are still you. You are still that circle. Now, imagine a smaller circle within you is your belief system. If you think that letting go of that belief system means you are losing a part of you, it's harder to change the belief. Just know that it is okay to let go of any belief system, and by letting go of it, you are not losing anything. You are transforming.

So let's talk about the power of an empty mind. People typically have very busy minds, so making space in your mind is beneficial. You may not know this, but when your mind is not busy working, your immune system is optimized. Healing is constantly taking place, but when you are doing nothing, healing happens even more effectively.

When I say, "healing is constantly taking place," you may be wondering what I mean. Let's say you have a cut on your hand. The cut will turn into a scab automatically. You don't have to say any special prayer or go through any ritual. It happens naturally, just like waking up in the morning. You go to sleep at night and the next day, the cut has turned into a scab. That's proof that healing is constantly taking place.

As I said, when you are doing nothing, that is when healing is optimized. Pay attention to this invisible power that's already in place. When you are not thinking, no emotions are interfering with your system. For example, when you are angry, a hormone called noradrenalin gets released, and that can be toxic to your system. When your mind is empty and open, it is not interfering with this healing process. When you do not think, there is no stress and no stress is a good thing for your mind and for your body. By creating space in your mind, you are optimizing the healing process. So emptying your mind is really a gift to your self.

This reminds me of a Zen retreat I went on thirty years ago in which I emptied both my mind and body for maximum healing. When I was on that retreat, I didn't eat anything. I just drank a gallon of water a day. By doing this I realized how much energy and time I was spending eating and processing food. The day feels a lot longer when you don't eat because when your body and mind are empty, your consciousness is clear. In a way, Zen can be considered a thought fasting practice for your mind to help it function better. When your body and mind are empty, the path to your soul opens.

Dealing with Attachment

Many of us have attachments, and sometimes, excessive attachments. This is the opposite of having an empty mind. For example, some people have excessive attachment to material things. They lose a favorite bag or watch and view it as a total disaster. Others find it difficult to deal with the loss of inherited objects, viewing it as a loss of part of their life. Some people have an attachment to a special person. For example, they may think that since they have been learning a lot from their mentor, they will not be able to resolve issues on their own when he or she is gone. However, things do not happen by accident. If their mentor is gone, it is because they are ready to be independent.

A former client had a special attachment to her husband of forty years. She had a tough life until she met her husband. Her life with her husband was great. When he passed away, she was devastated by the loss and felt that she had nothing left from their time together. That's one way of looking at it, but she could also choose to focus on all that she learned and gained in those forty years.

Some business owners have an attachment in their business. I know of a business owner who had a fear of losing a specific employee because his performance was excellent. When you focus on fear, you end up attracting fear. So as a result, this business owner lost the employee he was afraid of losing. However, after hiring someone new, who was just as good as his previous employee, the fear he initially felt disappeared. Once you know that when a door closes, another door opens, there isn't any need for strong attachments.

A strong belief system can be a form of attachment in your mind. Everybody has belief systems, but do you realize how many people fight over their different beliefs? For example, many of the wars going on in the world are rooted in differences in religious beliefs. This is where spirituality is different from religion. Being spiritual entails the ability to accept differences in beliefs. It means that people are ok with the fact that different people believe differently. There is no one standard in the world that says what is right and what is wrong. It's different for each person, each community. By knowing this, you can build a healthy distance from your belief systems. And beliefs can be changed to better serve your life.

Speaking of belief systems, sometimes your mind is conditioned to believe certain things from past events. Let's say when you were a child you were punished every time you decided to quit something, whether it was a musical instrument or sports team. Your Dad called you a quitter. Since then, you think that quitting is a bad thing. Now, you have a job that you don't like. Deep down, you know that you cannot stay there and shine. However, due to your past, you hear your father's voice in your mind saying, "Don't be a quitter." When you were told something repeatedly as a child, your mind gets conditioned. You can't help but let it affect your decisions. If you feel that this is happening to you, it is time to let go of this conditioning.

The process of letting go of conditioning or attachment doesn't happen instantly. It's not like you practice Zen for the first time for 10 minutes and then all of your past conditioning, beliefs, and attachments are gone. But with practice, you can enjoy this state of emptiness in your mind. At least for that moment, you will feel like time is forever and your mind is at peace. When your mind is empty and peaceful, your mental and physical health are optimized and your mind is ready to receive inspiration. That's the power of a clear mind.

I hope that by now you understand the power of emptiness and the benefit of creating a calm, spacious mind. Space leaves room for inspiration and resting your mind helps it recharge for more creativity and productivity. When your mind is calm, healing occurs at its best. When your consciousness is clear, you are connected to your inner self and your Life GPS. So, take time regularly to turn your mind off in order to best live your life.

Example #5: Taka's Story
This is a story about a man named Taka who had been controlled by his domineering mother all his life. He eventually decided to break away from her and start on his own path. He was always interested in spirituality and decided to add a spiritual element to his construction and design business. He quickly earned over $5,000 extra by following his passion. Now he feels mentally free from his restrictive mother and his business is skyrocketing. By incorporating spirituality into his design business, he is now known to all his competitors for his unique business

approach. He is also a certified Spiritual Life Coach in my program, and often speaks and assists other new coaches. This shift happened when he examined his beliefs and realized his mother's control was not serving him and therefore decided to make a change. This was the best decision he ever made and after that, his life and business both got better.

Chapter Six

The Power of Letting Go

If you want to achieve inner piece, no matter where you are in life, the skill of letting go is a muscle that is necessary to develop. People in the West are trained to memorize facts, but don't get taught to develop the muscle of letting go. When you build this muscle, your inner peace will change dramatically. Learning to let go may feel a bit like mental whack-a-mole, but it is worth learning. For example, when there is a thought that is bothering you, if you know how to let it go, you will no longer be bothered by it. If you're upset and it is affecting you and everybody around you and you learn how to let go of the thought that is generating the emotion, then you can achieve the mental state you want whenever you want.

If you don't learn how to control your emotions, it could cost you your job or even your career. When you are sad and feeling helpless or powerless, you lose mental and physical energy. But if you know how to let go of the thought that is making you sad at least temporarily, then your body and mind recover and feel better and it will be a lot easier to tackle the issue at hand.

Sometimes extreme things happen in life that are hard to swallow. For example, your loved one dies or your marriage comes to an end. Yes, things happen in life, and these big events typically create strong emotions, but there is a way to deal with them. When you think about it, everything can be viewed simply as information, including your experiences. Whether the impact of the event is big or small, it is information for you. Sometimes, the information can be small, such as getting a parking ticket or realizing you forgot to bring your cell phone to work. Other times, the information can be big, such as the loss of a loved one or receiving a termination notice at work. Regardless, it is all information.

When this information reaches your brain, you run the information through your thoughts, expectations, and belief systems and then you choose a response. I want you to understand that you have the power to change your response. Sometimes things happen so fast that you have no time to change your response and that's ok. You can pre-program your response for next time when something similar happens. Most of the time, however, when you realize that everything is simply information and your emotional responses are the result of how you see things, then you will know that your response is a conscious choice you can change if you choose to.

Emotions occur internally, so by controlling how you process information, you can control your response. If you find that your initial response was not your best, you can take a closer look at what thoughts are generating that response. Once you do that, you can then choose to let go of a thought and pick a new thought that empowers you. Remember, it is your own thoughts that bring you down or up. When you have not built this mental muscle of letting go, your mental life can feel like a roller coaster and such mental instability doesn't serve anyone. If you do not learn how to let go, your mind will become heavier with time and life may stop being fun.

The letting go muscle works best when you practice it before something happens. If you read this and say, "This sounds like a good idea. I'll try to let go next time something happens," then when something does happen and you try it for the first time, you'll find that it's very hard to let the thought go. So it's best to practice Zen when there is nothing bothering you. Close your eyes and when something pops up in your head, let it go. The best time to practice is when things are the most peaceful. If you practice this on an everyday basis, when something bigger happens, it will be a lot easier to respond to it. Learning how to let go creates space in your mind. When you have constant thoughts, there isn't much space left in your mind so there is no room to receive inspiration. When your mind is jammed, especially with negative emotions and thoughts, it can cause a storm in your mind that affects your body as well. By learning how to let go of thoughts that generates emotions you don't want, your mind will function at its best.

Clinging strongly to certain thoughts and beliefs likely will not serve you. When you cling to a thought or belief system, it prevents you from thinking freely or receiving inspiration. We have an infinite amount of potential when we are not bound by limiting beliefs or thoughts. However, when we cling to some old belief system, we are forced to think within that box. People say, "Think outside the box." To do so you need to let go of certain thoughts and detach yourself from any thought to which you are strongly clinging.

I know of a business owner who clings to the idea that he needs to be able to do everything on his own and cannot delegate work to other people. That is a self-imposed rule that limits him. There are also many women in Japan and in other parts of the world that believe the man should say, "I love you" first. If you want to cling to this idea, that's ok. However, it has the potential of creating limits in your life. I have a female friend who proposed to her current husband and they are both very happy.

Have you ever had an experience when you are at work and you have a thousand things to do and just the thought of having to finish it all creates a storm in your brain? Changing your mindset and recognizing that you can only tackle one issue at a time may change your mental state, which may change your approach. When we have too many thoughts in our mind, it is almost like a recipe to lose control. By clearing some thoughts and then simply focusing on one thing at a time, you will be able to get a lot more done and be more efficient. So learning how to let a thought go will also help your task management.

When I used to work in a corporate environment, a trip to Tokyo headquarters was of the utmost importance. If we did not perform well in Tokyo, we would be sent home or replaced. Tokyo was always the center stage to show our performance, and what we showed in Tokyo represented the work that we did in the United States. A lot of my colleagues worked late hours and had many sleepless nights because they wanted to perform well. Interestingly, my coworkers who worked late hours and pushed too hard didn't necessarily perform well in Tokyo.

To perform my best, I would go for a long drive during the busiest week right before the trip. I know it may sound like I was doing something bad, but I found that was the best way for me to perform well. So I would grab a car and drive for an hour or so.

First, I would focus on letting my thoughts go. This alone could easily take half an hour, especially on busy office days. Once I relaxed and emptied my mind, I would start asking myself some creative questions to receive inspiration. When I asked myself questions, I imagined myself being open. By keeping my mind open, it allowed the inspiration to come, instead of working hard to get it to come to me. Always allow inspirations to come rather than trying to force them. Inspiration would come when I was most relaxed and least expecting it, so once again letting go was the key.

Once I received my inspiration, I would record it on my voice recorder. After a one-hour drive, I would receive enough inspiration to put my ideas into a PowerPoint presentation, and the rest was easy. Once I got going, entering the images and the information into the PowerPoint presentation normally took about a half hour. Then I would spend the next few hours making it look better. The drive worked well for me, as opposed to sitting in front of the computer for hours trying to squeeze something out of my mind when I didn't have enough oxygen in my brain!

I use this example to show you that Zen can be applicable in a fast-paced business environment, too. The Zen I would like to teach you is not meant to help you get away from reality, but to make your reality better.

By the way, you can do the same thing by going for a walk in nature. This often works even more effectively since by connecting with nature, your body and mind work better. I went for a drive instead of a walk because I didn't want anybody catching me taking a walk during a busy week!

I would like to talk a bit more about multi-tasking. Most of the world has tricked themselves into believing that they can do several things at the same time. The truth is that the mind can only do one thing at a time. If you don't hold on to that one thing long enough, your subconscious mind never has a chance to kick in and help you. What do I mean by that? When you want to receive inspiration on a subject, it is necessary to keep your focus on that subject long enough to receive inspiration. When you do this, your mind will be ready to receive the inspiration from your subconscious mind. If you switch every two minutes from one thought to the next to the next, like many people do when they multitask, you are not giving yourself a chance to receive inspiration.

I think it's time to change the way we view multitasking. Instead of trying to perform two or more tasks simultaneously or constantly switching back and forth, the new goal could be to focus on one thing at a time and not be overwhelmed by the fact that you have multiple tasks to complete. When you focus on one thing at a time, you tackle things on a deeper level. If your goal is to do quality work instead of just producing quantity, you will want to learn how to focus on one thing at a time. If you want to be promoted, the best way is to provide a better quality of work rather than simply getting things done. So to produce better results, focus on one thing at a time. The ability to let go of all other thoughts except the one you want to focus on is therefore the key to producing quality work. As such, I encourage my employees, especially when they are busy, to take 5-10 minutes to practice Zen.

To reiterate, we have all been trained to remember things, to memorize and hold onto things. But the opposite muscle is as effective or even more so in producing a positive outcome. Learn how to let go of thoughts and how to empty your mind. You will be surprised how that increases your productivity. When you let go of everything else and simply focus on the most critical thing at that moment, you will be surprised how clear, productive, and efficient you can be.

Example #6: Kaori's Story

There was a woman named Kaori who was struggling with her business. She had a big inventory of Shea Butter products and she wanted to get rid of it. Then she came across my Spiritual Life Coach program. She was so drawn to it that she decided to pause her business and sign up for the year-long Spiritual Life Coaching program and became a very active member.

After three months or so her husband told her, "You need to pick one. You either focus on getting rid of the inventory of the existing business, or you earn some money from this spiritual life coaching. What do you choose?" Logically, she knew she should get rid of the inventory because she was not yet making any money from spiritual life coaching. But in her heart, she wanted to pursue life coaching so she decided to listen to her Life GPS and let go of the belief that it wasn't a smart decision. She had been reading my newsletter for years and she knew the importance of listening to her intuition. In the next 30 days, she made $10,000 just by making the decision to make a living at a Spiritual Life Coaching business. Within 90 days, she made over $30,000, and she is now helping my

Spiritual Life Coach association as a trainer. Her lane change from the Shea Butter business to the Spiritual Life Coaching business made a world of difference to her finances and happiness. All of that happened just by listening to her intuition. Who would have thought she could make $30,000 in a few months? Her inner self knew it was coming and thus sent a message as the feeling of excitement.

Chapter Seven

The Power of Inspiration

Inspiration can impact your life in many ways. For instance, one inspired idea can make you a lot of money. An example is EBay. Back in the 1990s there was no dominant place to sell or buy used products online, so the founder of EBay received an inspiration to create such a place. It was the same for YouTube. The founders were looking for an easy way to share videos online. So these three young gentlemen came up with the idea for YouTube. A year later, Google bought it for $1.65 billion. This is "The American Dream" and it all starts with an inspiration. If you are lucky, one inspiration that pops into your head can bring you millions of dollars.

One inspiration can change the direction of your life dramatically. I can give you an own example from my own life. When I was about to leave the corporate world, I came across an article from an entrepreneur magazine that was talking about a business model that I had thought of starting a couple of years before. I was so busy with my corporate job that I hadn't done anything with it. I was shocked to learn that the business was already generating a few million dollars a year.

Just by reading that article, I was inspired to start my own business. I felt an electrifying sensation run through my body confirming that I had to start my own business. So the next thing I did was pick up a notebook and write: "Today I have made a decision to start my own business within the next three years." Guess what? Things moved a lot faster than my initial projection. Two months after setting the three-year timeline, I had set up my company, and six months later, I generated my first sales online. I officially resigned from my job eight months later. This is just one example of how a single inspiration can change the direction of your life dramatically. That inspiration worked out well for me, as I've been in business for 14 years now and it's going well. Best of all, I am much happier than I was in my corporate days. This is the best decision I have made in my life, and it all started with an inspiration I received by reading an article in a magazine.

Another possible effect of inspiration is creating instant happiness by shifting your mindset. I'll give you an example. There was a woman who was always busy doing something. She had a belief that she should always be in action and had to perform better than others. This mindset came from her dad, who gave her conditional love by approving of her only when she performed well. Years later, through reading books and attending self-help seminars, she started to hear things like, "love is the most important thing" or "being contributes to others more than doing." At first, she was confused hearing things that didn't match was she heard growing up. She decided to listen to her inner self as she learned to do in one of my seminars. As she did that, she experienced a sense of knowing that she didn't have to do anything to receive approval or prove her worthiness. Before the inspiration, she was constantly striving to perform better and to be accepted by her dad. However, with one inspiration, and with the message from her inner self, she was able to feel inner peace without having to earn it.

Inspiration can also lead to an increased income. For example, the first few years after starting my own business, I was doing internet marketing consulting, but my soul's interest was shifting to the spiritual. I couldn't make that shift easily because my business was based on internet marketing, not spirituality. At the time, I had twenty thousand subscribers who wanted to hear my internet marketing tips. Every time I talked about spirituality in my newsletters, some people complained and some unsubscribed. I began to fear losing my business, and as a result my mind resisted making the shift. One night, however, I had a spiritual experience. I went to bed early that night, and something woke me up. Upon waking, it felt like an energy had entered my body and I felt a spiritual, physical and emotional sensation unlike anything I had ever experienced before. I believe that was a nudge from the universe to assist me in making the shift to follow my heart. So I made the decision. I didn't know how to make the shift from internet marketing to a spiritual business, but I made the decision anyway.

Once you make a decision, things start to happen. A few weeks later, during a routine morning walk, out of nowhere I received an inspiration consisting of the words, "Life Optimization Consultant." With those keywords, I knew I could revamp my website completely and make the shift from internet marketing to spiritual life coaching. The following three to five days, I wrote around fifty pages to redo my website. When I made that shift, my business quadrupled in one year and my subscriber base went from twenty thousand to sixty thousand in a two-year period. This is one example of an inspiration changing the course of a business and resulting in increased income.

I hope that by now you are convinced of the power of inspiration. So what do you do to be able to receive inspiration? It's very simple - practicing Zen every day is the best way to start.

I already mentioned that my Zen experience started 30 years ago when I first attended a fasting and Zen retreat. Once I had the knowing that I am a soul and that my soul knows the answers to life questions, I became what some may call "addicted" to doing Zen daily. When you know that there is a place inside you where you can access deep wisdom and answers to questions about your life, wouldn't you want to keep that communication line open? So that's what I have been doing since I attended the fasting and Zen retreat many years ago.

Every time you face a critical decision, go inside yourself and practice Zen. Something good will happen, which will make you believe this concept even more.

The first step is to always empty your mind using Zen. Inspiration is a great example of the concept of working smarter, not harder. Some people strongly believe that you must work harder to be wealthy and happy, but that is not the case. When you know that one inspiration can change your life or bring you thousands or even millions of dollars, you will see life differently; Zen practice will have a whole new meaning to you.

There are other ways to receive inspiration. You don't necessarily have to sit with your eyes closed and meditate or practice Zen. I often use walking. That life optimization consultant story is an example. I wasn't looking for an answer. I was just walking, my mind clear, simply enjoying nature, and that created a good energy flow in my body and my mind. As such, I was able to receive inspiration.

Another activity that I enjoy is swimming. I love that there is no chance to talk or listen when I'm underwater. Swimming is an oxygen intensive sport, so while you are swimming, you are getting a lot of oxygen and your energy is moving throughout your body. Also, because humans are 70% water, when you are in the water, you can go into a special state. When I am swimming, I receive a lot of inspiration. Sometimes I even stop swimming so that I can write down my thoughts.

Hiking is also good. Being in nature, rather than surrounded by the concrete jungle, makes a big difference. When you hike, you receive sunshine and energy. Hiking is also another whole-body exercise, which can give you a lot of energy flow. When you walk or exercise for at least a half hour, that's when you start to burn fat, and your mind starts to be clear. I know that I feel better after the first half hour. That's the time when your inspirational door is wide open.

Just after exercising is another excellent time to receive inspiration. Back in my corporate days, I was busy during the week. However, I made it to the gym every weekend for exercise. I would walk, swim, soak in the hot tub, and end my exercise with a relaxing steam sauna. With my whole body filled with oxygen and energy flowing throughout, I would be in a good mental state. As I drove back home, I would listen to self-help CDs and because of my relaxed mental and physical state, I received a lot of inspiration. I often listened to self-help CDs at other times as well, but there was something different when I listened to them after the gym. What was most different was my mental state. I realized that the best time to receive inspiration was when I was in the best physical and mental state. Since then, I only listen to self-help CDs when I am in my optimal state. I apply the same rule when I am reading a book. I do not read a book when I am burnt out or tired. I read mostly in the morning when my mind is clear and active. If I read when I'm tired, then I miss out on receiving inspiration, so I always read books or listen to audio CDs when I am at my peak.

Because your mind opens up when you are in an optimal physical and mental state, you need to be careful what you expose yourself to during that time. Don't listen to abusive language or watch violent TV shows when you are in an optimal physical and mental state. It's always good to be careful what information you send to your mind, but especially when you are at your most receptive. When you exercise, your body wants water and nutrients instead of junk food. The same goes for the mind. The mind is also open first thing in the morning and right before you go to bed so be especially careful what you listen to or what you watch at those times as well.

Listening to soothing music or a good Zen CD while you are falling asleep is a good idea. You could also record your own positive affirmations in a soft voice. However, only record when you are feeling 100%. If you record when you are feeling negative or doubtful, that vibration will show up in your voice. If you listen to that over and over, you will stay where you are instead of absorbing the affirmation. So keep in mind that when you listen to audio or watch a video, you are not only getting the content, you are also receiving vibrations. If you are listening to an audio from someone who has a positive outlook, then you receive that higher vibration and it helps you go from where you are to the next level.

Lastly, when you are sending messages to your mind, send messages that affirm the things you want, not what you don't. For example, if you keep repeating to yourself, "I do not want to be poor," your mind deletes the word "not" and just receives the word "poor." So instead of saying, "I don't want to be poor," say, "I choose to be wealthy." Even better is something like, "I am enjoying my wealth," or "I am enjoying abundance," because those seem even more real. As I mentioned, I listen to programs or read books for stimulation, inspiration, and conditioning. Just like exercising the body every day, we need to do the same thing for the mind.

Example #7: Aya's Story

There was a woman named Aya who was always stressed out, working around the clock for an advertising agency. Exhausted when she came to my workshop, she wasn't sure where her life was going. It was not good for her spiritual growth to stay in the company that was depleting her energy, but since that was her source of income, she believed she could not just quit her job. Eventually, she came to a seven-day retreat I held in Italy, and that was long enough for her to receive inspiration about what she wanted to do with her life. On the last day, she loudly declared to all the participants that she would quit her job and follow her spiritual path.

Soon after she started to pursue this path, she met her "soul mate" and within a few months they got married. I know a few months may seem like a short time to decide on marriage, but for people who know how to listen to their inner truth, it's long enough. That was over two years ago, and they are still madly in love. Before this, she wasn't sure where her life was going and she didn't know what to do. There were things she had been interested in spiritually, but she had never known where to start or where her talent lay. She just knew that working at the advertising agency was depleting her, so she decided to leave the job. When she signed up for a spiritual trip to India, she met her soul mate. All this was made possible by the decision she made to follow her inspiration, change lanes, and approach life differently.

Chapter Eight

The Power of Leverage

In the previous chapter, I talked about the power of inspiration. Isn't it exciting to know that one inspiration can change many aspects of your life instantly? In this chapter, I would like to talk about the power of leverage. What do I mean by that? Here are some examples: If you master how to empty your mind, and are able to achieve inner peace whenever you desire, that skill stays with you for the rest of your life. If you master how to receive a message from your life GPS anytime you want to, that skill stays with you always. Also, if you master how to receive an inspiration when you want it, that skill stays with you as long as you want. That's the power of leverage. It does take some time to master some of these techniques I teach in this book, but once you do, that skill will be yours forever. You will enjoy an enhanced quality of life for the rest of your life. Would you be willing to spend ten minutes of your day mastering these skills?

Many people think that sitting quietly is a waste of time, and they think that practicing Zen is time spent away from what we should be doing, but it's not the case. If you could receive an inspiration that enhances your life, would you spend 10 minutes a day on it? What if you could always make the right decision every time, even the critical decisions, and just spend 10 minutes a day doing it?

What if you have absolute knowing what you are here for? A lot of people search their meaning and purpose in life. If you have absolute knowing as to who you are, what you are, what you are here for, what you are doing for your life, then to some people, that's ultimate happiness. Let's say in a week, months, or sometimes years, if you can get to that point where you have the absolute knowing of what you are and who you are, is that a worthwhile investment?

I know what I am here for, and I am blessed. I am so happy since I have discovered what I am here for. Every second of life is an absolute joy and you can be there, too. That's what this book is about. To know what you are here for, and the only way is to go inside.

Once you have the knowing, you can't go back to not knowing. The know-how, or wisdom that you get through the Zen experience will stay with you for life. Once you learn that process of emptying your body or emptying your mind and receiving inspiration, you can keep this skill and enjoy its benefit for the remainder of your life. Abraham Lincoln once said if he had 10 minutes to cut a tree down, he'd spend 8 minutes sharpening the ax. This is the right mindset to get what you want out of life. Ten minutes of daily Zen is really an act of sharpening your ax. Once you know the concept of leverage, your priority for life will change.

You become less stressed when you know how to deal with your inner self, and you can experience a life of no fear or less fear. This is what you can get by using this mind emptying technique. This is a better or more efficient way of living your life, the choice between days and weeks of agony or fear, versus 10 minutes of Zen and you have the knowing that you are on the right spiritual path. It's a choice between a life of searching versus a life of knowing. Your life changes once you know how to harness this new tool. That tool is something that you don't need to go out and pay a lot of money for. You only allocate a portion of your time.

A lot of people say, "I don't have time for Zen." That's not true.

We all have time. We just need to reprioritize. Other people say, "I am too busy for Zen." To that I will say that's exactly why you should do Zen. I understand it's not easy to start doing something without seeing the visible outcome immediately, but patience is the key, my friend. All the achievements in the world come by patience and daily effort. Plus, 10 minutes a day is not going to kill you. Hundreds of thousands of people have started the Zen practice with my guidance in Japan, and I have gotten zero complaints. No one has returned to say, "I lose too much time practicing Zen," or "my life has gotten worse since I started Zen." On the contrary; practicing Zen has no side effects or any physical damages. It simply gives you an enhanced quality of life. You can achieve that for no cost, zero interest, no payment, and for only 10 minutes a day.

The more you practice, the easier it gets to empty your mind, and the easier it is to receive inspiration. Most people, before they even start practicing Zen, might think this is something they must work hard to achieve. It's not that hard, if you practice every single day. I have seen people seeing benefits in the first week, and many start to see a change in them within a few weeks. To get the most out of your life, it's best to learn how to get the most out of your mind, since everything happens from within. Zen is an effective tool, to get the most out of your mind; however, it is not the only element.

To assist you in understanding this further, I would like to talk about belief systems, and how critical those are to your mind and to your life. For example, my friend Mike can manifest a close parking spot whenever he goes to the store. What makes it possible? It's the belief that he can. He can also wake up within five minutes of the time he sets for himself. How is that possible? Because he believes that he can. That's the power of belief. You have probably heard of placebo effects. It has been proven, that in most instances, people can get almost as much relief from a placebo as they get from real medicine. That is another example of the power of pure belief. As it works with smaller things in your life, you start to trust it more and believe that you can change bigger things. Zen will grow in its power as you practice it more, and the same goes for your belief system.

Take for instance my friend and business mentor, John Assaraf, from the movie "The Secret." He had a lot of health issues when he was young; he was taking over 20 pills a day, and was losing control over his life. He learned to believe in the power of mind and the power of the belief system, so he started doing affirmations several times a day. Within three months, he was no longer taking any pills. Things like that can happen to anybody. That's the power of the belief system.

How people build their belief system is different for each person, but a lot of people build it unconsciously. They are built in their childhood, by their parents. It's not that parents are doing something bad; in many cases, parents are doing what they are doing unconsciously, because their belief system has also been installed by their parents. From your perspective, when you are young and kind of helpless, your life is subject to your parents' decisions. So you are in the perfect environment to have your belief system influenced. I believe that if you are reading this book, it is no coincidence. It might just be the best time to revisit your belief system, and make sure that the ones you decide to keep, is going to serve a good purpose.

In this information age, it is important to make a careful and conscious decision as to which information to believe and which not to. Let's say you are watching television and a commercial about sugar comes on. It is important to note that advertisers promote their products with the most attractive visual effects, working hard to make as many sales as possible. It is their job to sell the product. Your optimal health is not their primary goal when creating the advertisement. At the same time, there are articles on the Internet that explain the risk of sugar. When you have two different reports, just go inside and ask your inner self which might be true. Be careful not to expose yourself to TV commercials with all their visual and sound effects. By doing so, you are installing this information in your mind, including your subconscious mind, which has more influence than you imagine. Be selective with the information you expose yourself to.

More people pay attention to what they eat today; however, they pay less attention to what they send to their mind. Energy, messages, music, you can't be too conscious of what you get in your mind, because that influences the nature of your mind, more than you can imagine. Your mind is like a reality generation center. Everything in the world started in somebody's mind. By knowing that, you want to nurture your mind with good stuff. When both your conscious mind and subconscious mind are filled with good thoughts, intentions and positive thinking will be your reality. Today can be the day you start paying attention to what you watch, what you hear, who to hang out with, and what books to read. At the end of the day, just as a checkpoint, empty your mind and listen to your soul and see what served you. Then you will have the knowing. You may not get an answer or the knowing on the day you want, but you will shortly.

You must be patient, because even though the answer is always there, it takes some time for you to be ready to receive it. When you are ready, you will hear it. Just as when the students are ready, a teacher shows up.

This whole process of mastering Zen or nurturing your mind is an ongoing effort. It is a lifestyle. Do you ever go to the gym for a workout and say, "I am done with fitness for the rest of my life?" The same goes for training, or nurturing your mind. Most of you work hard to be able to learn your favorite sports, like baseball, basketball or surfing. However, for meditation, many try it and after ten minutes say, "I can't meditate." Watch out when you say, "I can't meditate," Your mind is listening, and that could become your reality. So you want to choose your words carefully because once you say it, it's even more powerful. So, if you want to build a new belief system, think it, say that, and repeat that over and over. Whatever you say, your subconscious mind is listening, and when the subconscious mind receives that, it starts making it happen.

Now it's okay if you say bad words from time to time. We all stumble in this area. However, if you do it over and over, that becomes your belief system, and your identity. As soon as that happens, you start attracting people with similar energy, and you don't want that. As long as you nurture your mind with words, thoughts and beliefs that resonate with your soul, you will be true to who you are, and your happiness starts from there.

Real Life Story #8
The next story is about a woman whose life and business wasn't working at all, but with just a simple change of her self-image, she started generating $100,000 in sales a month. She was a VP in her dad's business, but the business wasn't going well, and when she signed up for my personal consultation, she told me she had spent $10,000 on online campaigns but they were not producing any results. When I listened to her entire story, I realized that it wasn't just about business. Her employees were embezzling company inventory, and as a result their organization was falling apart. I sensed that all these issues were rooted in her low self-esteem instilled by her father. She grew up being told by her father, "that's why you are no good." That was deeply installed in her belief system. I told her the problem she had was not about business consulting, and I suggested that she come to my three-day spirituality and business workshop. Through the workshop, her self-image changed dramatically, and she went home totally empowered.

A few months after the workshop I received an email from her which said everything had turned around positively, since the workshop and for the first time in the history of her company, they had reached $100,000 sales in one month. What happened was very simple. She went back to work with confidence, and a determination to make things better. When you make decisions that ignite change, interesting things start to happen. The first thing she did was hire a new employee. At the time she hired her, she had no idea that this employee was psychic. The new employee started telling her everything that was going on with the other employees who were embezzling inventory. With the psychic's help, she was able to collect all the evidence of their embezzlement, and decided to let them go, and replaced them with new and good employees. Now she had a great team working for her. Consequently, she used the team as well as her own creativity to increase the sales to $100,000.

About a year later, she emailed me again and told me that her business had grown to $200,000 a month in sales. All of this happened by the change of her image. As I said, all of the change happens with your mind first. This is a great example of that.

Chapter Nine

The Power of Mind Control

When I use the term mind control, I am not talking about a super power or brainwashing. Rather, I mean it quite literally. When you control your mind, you control your life. If you do not take charge of your own mind, you let others control you. It's critical to manage your mind, because everything begins there. Fortunately, your mind is like a muscle you can train, and there are five skills that you can work on to develop it.

The first is the skill of pivoting. If you know basketball, you understand what it means to pivot. You try to pass to one teammate, and if it doesn't work, you pivot. With one foot still planted, you turn around, look the other way, and then you pass. We can also pivot in our minds. Maybe you feel stuck with something and it feels like life is closing in on you. However, when you pivot and you are able to see the same situation from a different perspective, you can see a bright future. This ability to pivot, especially when things do not seem to be working out, is critical. Just ask yourself, "Is this true?" When you see the same situation from a different angle, what seems so real and desperate may not be so bad after all.

The second skill is letting go. When you have a thought that is restricting your spirit, depleting your energy, or creating negative emotion, you might need to let it go. Letting go requires practice as I discussed earlier, but this is also like a muscle that can be trained. You likely never had a chance to learn this skill in your childhood, but you can develop it now without going anywhere or paying any money. Once you develop the skill of letting go, you can be free of anything that is binding, restricting, or slowing you down, which is tremendously beneficial.

Number three is the skill of using your imagination. Imagination is so very powerful. Einstein once said, "Imagination is more important than knowledge." He was correct. Information is limited, but imagination is infinite. Today we live in an information age, and we have access to so much data, but it is still not infinite. Life can be thought of as a game of how to utilize your imagination from all the available information. Imagination can go beyond anyone's knowledge. When you develop your ability to imagine or create something, it can take you in a whole new direction and open all kinds of possibilities.

The fourth skill is the ability to trust. When things don't go the way you want, it's easy to start doubting yourself and your life. That's the opposite of trust. However, when you truly believe that everything happens for a good reason in terms of your spiritual growth, you can believe that there is light at the end of the tunnel. And the more you believe, the easier it is to find the light. Whether you believe you can find the light or not, that will become your reality, as we previously discussed. So the ability to trust, despite fear and doubt, is one of the most important skills to develop.

There is a popular book and movie I mentioned earlier called "The Secret" that talks about the Law of Attraction. Millions of people watched the video or read the book and started using affirmations in their daily routines, but not everybody got the same results. Why? It comes down to a lack of trust. When you have 100% faith and trust in what you are saying and in what you are doing the affirmations for, then they are much more likely to come to fruition. That is the way it works. So the ability to trust is the fuel to realizing your desires.

Finally, number five is the ability to act. When you do affirmations, the universe usually brings you the opportunity to obtain the thing instead of the thing itself. So to get the result you want, you have to act on the opportunity presented to you. When you hear the word action, you may feel like it is an external, physical thing and it's not. The action itself could be physical, but the decision to take an action is internal. This skill can change the course of your life dramatically. A lot of people have great ideas, but not everybody acts on them. Most people would like to be doers, but to be a doer you need to make the internal decision first. So the decision to act is crucial to get what you want out of life.

Once you develop this skill, it can become a habit. When you come up with an idea, you act on it. When you take quick decisive action, you often get good results. Your brain will begin to associate pleasure with taking action immediately. Then you will be unstoppable.

This skill might not be easy to develop at first. It might take some time and patience. It's like a car—once it starts going, it gets easier to accelerate. The same applies to being in action. Once you develop this skill, it won't be too hard to maintain. So whatever inspiration you receive, whatever great idea you come up with, act on it to make it happen. When you do this, you'll be a step closer to your dream.

Again, you can't be too careful in choosing what messages you take in. There are a ton of advertisements out there that want you to buy their product, and not necessarily because it's good for you. For example, when soda companies advertise, they attempt to trick your mind so that you will like their product. When you turn on the television, every commercial has a goal. They pay billions to broadcast that commercial and they need to get their money back for their investment. So the information that's presented, especially visual and audio, goes deep into your subconscious unless you establish some distance from it. If you are not able to establish this distance, the information that constantly enters your mind can negatively affect you. So unless you know how your mind works and you make a conscious decision to control and protect it, it can be controlled by others. It's critical to understand how the mind works and to be able to control it, so you can be in control of your life.

A good example of mind control is a song from a commercial that you may have seen when you were younger. You remember it because of the visuals, the words and the music, the cadence, and the repetition. That's how songs get stuck in your mind. Every word and picture in those commercials is painstakingly thought out to maximize the impact on your mind. For example, remember the Zest soap commercials? The campaign with the jingle "You're not fully clean unless you're Zestfully clean!" was clearly effective given that I still remember it immediately years later.

When a person is in a toxic environment, that person becomes depleted or depressed. A question I have heard countless times throughout my coaching career is: "Should I stay or should I go?" My answer is always the same: listen to your body. When the toxic environment depletes your energy and you start to see physical symptoms, then it's a sure sign from your soul that it's time to leave the environment. It may not be easy. You might say, "I have a family," or "My pay is not bad and I am not sure I can find a new job." Remember, the universe never makes your environment toxic until there is a new path for you. That's how the universe works. So if the environment is depleting you, it is a nudge from the universe to change lanes.

Sometimes the environment is toxic because the Universe is testing you to see if you have the guts to leave the place that doesn't serve you. Sometimes people stay in a toxic place out of fear of leaving or they prefer the uncomfortable familiar place to an unfamiliar place. But when an environment is eating up your energy and depleting you, instead of trying to control your mind and finding a way to think positive in the negative environment, move on to a new environment. You can learn how to control your thoughts in other circumstances. You don't need a toxic environment to learn to control your mind. If anything, it only makes it more difficult.

Daily Conditioning

Daily conditioning is critical in learning to control your mind. Start your day with a positive book or audio recording. Pick something that uplifts your soul. Likewise, what you think about before going to bed is critical because that's the thought you will wake up with. When you go to bed with a positive mindset, it's nurtured during your sleep, so you will wake up thinking positively. You can also reinforce that positive thinking by re-reading what you read the night before. This is a powerful method of conditioning.

Another thing that I do for daily conditioning is listening to an audio program. Reading can give you much information, but when you listen to an audio program, it not only gives you information, it also gives you energy. Have you ever listened to an audio that has informative information, but you don't enjoy listening to it because the voice does not carry any energy? Perhaps at the same time, there is another audio program that completely energizes you. Find a program that is both informative and energizing. Once you find a program like that, you can listen to that as part of your daily conditioning.

Example #9: Kana's Story
A woman named Kana was in the IT business and felt stuck. She was always stressed, employees kept leaving, and it felt like everything was falling apart. Things were not going well with her partner either so she wanted to know where her life was heading. After attending my workshop, she saw the light, almost in a magical way. I told her that when things are not going the way you want, it is time to change lanes, even though it might be painful.

She understood the concept, and after recognizing the need to trust and let go, she was able to use her imagination to pivot and make changes. Then almost immediately, she was shown a way to leave the IT Company where she'd been working. She felt freedom, and soon enough she came across the concept of social entrepreneurism. Now she is running a social entrepreneur business in Asia and is truly happy.

None of this would have been possible if she had held on to her previous environment. The decision to change lanes created new possibilities. Opportunities are always there when one door closes.

Chapter Ten

The Power of an Optimized Body

In the previous chapter, we talked about the importance of controlling your mind. Truly controlling the mind also requires controlling the body, as they are inextricably interconnected. To control your body you need to be intentional about three things: what and how you eat, how you exercise, and how you rest.

Let's discuss number one, what and how you eat. What you eat drastically changes how you feel physically as well as mentally. When you go to the grocery store there are thousands of foods and products made with chemicals, including additives and preservatives. These are meant to make products last longer, not to keep you healthy.

There are many toxins in food and in the environment so detoxing is critical to keeping a good physical state. There are a lot of detoxifying products available, including detox teas and herbs that I take on a regular basis.

If you want your body to work its best, you will need to rid your body of toxic substances. I often share what I eat and what I do to detox on my website: **www.kaziso.com**.

Since humans are 70% water, the key for maintaining health is to keep replacing old water with new fresh water. The best time to rehydrate your body is in the morning because the morning is when your body naturally wants to cleanse. It's best to start your day with luke-warm water. Your body will keep detoxing as long as you consume water, organic fruits, raw vegetables or non-caffeine herbs. These are all water-based foods that help with detoxification. The moment you eat processed or cooked foods that contain chemicals, preservatives or unnatural products, the detox and healing process stops and your body will start trying to process those other products. It takes a lot of energy to process toxins so the body must stop cleaning and healing itself.

As such, it's best to start your day with fresh luke-warm water in the morning. By doing this, your body will simply start cleansing itself automatically. Warm water is better than cold because your body temperature is lower in the morning, and when your body temperature is lower, your immune system is compromised. If your organs become colder, your body temperature will go even lower and then your body will have to work hard to bring your body temperature back up. The warm water can be either the same temperature as your body or a little higher, because by increasing your body temperature, the body will turn on.

Many people in the Western world start their day with coffee. Coffee contains caffeine, which is a very strong substance. It wakes up your mind and body temporarily but after the effects wear off, it has a rebound effect which make you feel more tired. Caffeine is a very strong and addictive substance, and it will stop the detox process almost immediately. For that reason, I do not drink coffee or consume caffeine on a regular basis. Staying away from caffeine also helps my business. I live in the U.S and have clients in Japan, and sometimes I Skype with them at night in California. If I start my day with coffee, I will be burnt out by evening. I therefore avoid coffee and caffeine at almost all cost when I will be talking with my clients at night so I can be at my best even in the evening.

Our bodies often end up being overly acidic from eating today's food, so alkalizing your body is also a great way to start your day. That's another reason why I start my day by squeezing a lemon into warm water. If you want, you can do a quick experiment and see how you feel when you drink caffeine and sugar versus lemon water. Drink coffee and sugar every day for seven days and see how you feel at the end of each day. Do the same thing with lemon water. Drink the lemon water every day and see how you feel at the end of the day. By alkalizing your body, you will feel less tired and your mental state will be improved.

Avoid processed sugar as much as you can as it takes away nutrients from your body. In addition, sugar is very addictive. If you feel addicted to sugar, avoid it for a week or two to neutralize your body. It's ok to please your tongue and give yourself a sweet taste every now and then. However, eating sugar daily will compromise your health and your mental state. Many people go for coffee and sugar when they want to focus, but a healthy and effective alternative is freshly squeezed lemon juice into warm water.

Try to also avoid "heavy foods." Heavy foods are the kinds that make your body feel heavy that day or the following day. Meats, alcohol and dairy products are examples of "heavy foods." If you eat a lot of meat, your stomach or digestive system starts to feel heavy. Dairy products, including cheese, stay in your stomach longer than most vegetables and fruits.

What would happen if you went without alcohol, meat, or dairy products for a week? Try it as an experiment. Notice how light your body becomes. If you practice Zen meditation along with this experiment of going vegetarian for a week, you will feel a significant difference.

If you would like to try an extreme test, try an even more restrictive diet for seven days. No meat, no alcohol, no caffeine, no dairy and no junk food or processed food, and avoid sugar as much as you can. Instead, just consume a lot of raw food, vegetables, fruits and nuts. The following week, eat meat, drink alcohol and eat junk food for seven days, and notice the difference in your body and in your mental state. Do not do this experiment without consulting your doctor. If you have any special conditions, you might not want to try this. If you are healthy, this experiment will reveal how different diets affect your body.

If you go vegetarian for three weeks, very often your body will not have the craving for meat anymore and your body will feel lighter. When you feel lighter and also practice Zen, sometimes you might not even feel your body or you might forget that you are in your body. That's the ideal condition. The information that I am sharing here is for that exact purpose. When your body is lighter, your mind will be lighter.

I shared earlier I went on a fasting Zen retreat many years ago. Fasting has three purposes: 1) to detox 2) to allow your body to focus on healing 3) to assist your body in becoming light so that your mind can focus.

This is a prime example of when more is not necessarily better. In the Western world, a lot of people think that more food is better. In the East, however, many people think that, just as animals fast when they are ill, people also recover more quickly if they fast when they are ill. In addition to allowing the body to focus on healing, fasting can help you to focus more effectively and therefore, it allows your mind to work much better. When your mind works better, your life works better.

How you eat is just as important as what you eat. Chewing well is important because by chewing a lot you release natural enzymes and you end up eating slower. You spend more time eating, which gives your body enough time for your sugar level to go up so that you have time to notice feeling full. When you eat quickly, your body doesn't know if it's had enough or not. When you chew enough, the enzymes in the food make it easier to digest and you will not need to spend as much energy on it.

Recently I spoke with a receptionist at a chiropractic office. She said she starts her day with coffee and doesn't drink water often, partly because she thinks water has no taste. I asked her: "Do you please your body or please your tongue?" It's a simple but deep question. Many people choose to please the tongue and end up eating things that don't serve the body. If happiness is created in your mind and your physical state affects your mental state, then your mental state is largely affected by what you eat. I highly recommend making the choice to please your body with some regularity instead of constantly pleasing your tongue. You don't have to change everything you are doing immediately. Simply try applying new eating habits one at a time.

I told you that on the seven day Zen retreat I did, all I had was drinking water. I think it was the last day when they served a little bit of cooked vegetables. No salt. No sauce, simply vegetables. I was amazed at how delicious the cabbage, onion, and other vegetables were without salt or sauce. My body and tongue had been neutralized by not having any chemically processed toxic food for seven days. Once you experience something like this, it will forever change your concept of what true gourmet is.

Now, let's discuss number two, how you exercise. There are about 20 items on my daily exercise list. In addition to my diet and detox methods, I also often post information about my exercises with photos on my website.

Stretches and yoga are great ways to listen to your body. When your body is tense, you want to relax it so you can be flexible before you start your day. While doing stretches or exercises, you'll want to pay attention to your breathing. You'll want to breathe slowly so that you get into a good mental state and are able to focus during the day.

Also, by breathing deeply, you are supplying oxygen to your body, which it needs. It's a good idea to try to have as much oxygen as possible before a meeting or important speaking engagement. Breathe slowly or take a deep breath and then hold it for a few seconds or longer. Just by paying attention to your breathing, you can increase your productivity because productivity is tied to oxygen consumption and your brain consumes a lot of oxygen. The brain is said to consume as much as 20% of the oxygen in your body, so it's beneficial to supply ample oxygen to your brain before critical moments. Being conscious of your breathing and your oxygen supply is critical to achieving optimal health and mental state.

When you control your breathing, you also control your brainwaves. Many people wake up in the morning and the first thing they do is look at their email, which basically opens up Pandora's box. This is not a good way to start your day. When you spend enough time preparing your mind and body to start your day, you can better control your mind, emotions, and brainwaves. If you are presented with unexpected emails from angry customers and you have spent enough time clearing your mind and body, you can handle the situation much more effectively.

When you start your day by sitting at your computer and working, without making time for exercising or breathing, it's easier to burn out. If you exercise, get enough oxygen, and prepare your mind for the events of the day, when you do get to work, you will last a lot longer. I have tried this many times myself and I share this with all my clients in Japan. They all give me great feedback and say they work better and are much more productive when they follow this routine before working.

In addition to being unpleasant, any physical tension in one part of your body will create another tension in another part. That's how your body compensates for what's not working. It's important to pay attention to your tissues and muscles every day so that you know what physical state you are in. It's always good to catch any issues early instead of waiting until the situation becomes more severe and difficult to treat.

During a busy week when there is a lot going on in my office, I sometimes see employee's energy change. I often see their energy going up through their shoulders and neck instead of flowing smoothly throughout the body. When I see that, I tell them to take a five or ten-minute break to practice Zen. Many people want to skip this process of relaxation and go right to work. While it may seem like an inefficient use of time, real efficiency is being consistent and productive.

Massage is also a great way to relax your body and mind, but it does take money and time. As part of my routine, I work with a tennis ball or a foam roller for 5-10 minutes a day. There are a lot of products and information out that that can help relax your body and mind for a low cost.

Finally, number three is rest. As I mentioned before, when you are resting or in a relaxed state, healing is taking place. Even during the workday you can find time to empty your mind and body. Just by taking five or ten minutes, you can work better and for a lot longer. Many people wait until the last minute or until their system shuts down to rest. I suggest resting proactively instead of reactively.

The ultimate rest is sleep. Do your best to get quality sleep. If you drink a lot of beer and then sleep, you will not get the best quality sleep. The same goes for eating heavy food. That will not give you quality sleep either. The next morning your body feels heavier, and it almost feels as if your blood is flowing more slowly.

Let's say you get seven or eight hours of sleep daily. The time at which you go to bed makes a difference. You probably know from experience that going to bed at 10pm will give you better sleep than going to bed at 2am. Your body goes into a deep sleep state a few hours after you go to sleep. Ideally, you get to this deep sleep state around midnight. So going to bed around 10pm will serve your body in terms of getting quality sleep. Another benefit of going to bed early is being able to wake up more easily early the next morning. It is peaceful and quiet when you wake up before the rest of the world. It is much easier to clear your mind at 5am when it is just you and the universe as opposed to at 8am when your cell phone starts to go off.

I mentioned earlier that I practice Zen every morning and start my day with exercise. If you wake up at 8am or 9am and you must be at work within half an hour, then it's harder to practice Zen or have the focus that you need. But if you wake up early, your day begins before anybody else. You have the luxury to be by yourself to take the time you need to clear your mind and do some exercises to wake your body up. It's a great way to start your day as opposed to waking up late and rushing around.

Children are great examples of resting when fatigued. When a young child gets tired they simply lie down and go to sleep wherever they are. Adults should do that, too, if circumstances allow it. Many people feel guilty about resting, but the reason for fatigue is that your body needs rest and healing. When you keep resisting or postponing rest, something bigger will hit you. Sometimes it's catching a cold or picking up an illness. Some people want to prove that they are a "superman" or "superwoman" by resisting fatigue. This does not serve you. Be easy on your body. When you keep pushing your body, there will always be push-back. Also, inspiration doesn't come to a fatigued mind. So keep your physical container, also referred to as your body, healthy so it can receive the inspiration you want. If you wait too long in your fatigued state, and you stop paying attention to the signals from your body, it guarantees an impaired body. So do not wait too long to take the rest your body needs.

When you put off resting, your body stops healing and that can create a whole number of problems. Remember that sleep is the best healing system. Just by getting quality sleep or rest when you need it, your body will do its job. If your happiness is a priority, it's important to take resting and sleeping seriously.

I'd like to end this chapter talking about cycles. As you listen to your mind, it allows you to better listen to your body. As you listen to your body and do what it tells you, it in turn helps you to listen to your mind. It's a spiraling effect where both get better and better, or the reverse occurs. So do your best to stay in a positive and healthy cycle to best support your body and mind.

One of the first success coaches in Japan over a century ago once said, "You are a consciousness or a soul that's governing your body and mind, so life is really about your soul managing your body and mind smartly and effectively." If you have that trinity - your soul, body, and mind - in harmony, you will be in good shape. When your body is not working well, then your mind will also not work well. Therefore, you will have less efficient access to your soul and your Life GPS.

When your mind is too busy, it creates stress in your mind and the stress will affect your physical state. Similarly, when your energy is not flowing smoothly in your body, it affects your mind, therefore affecting your communication with your inner self. You know from experience that your mind can be stagnant and that often comes from stagnant energy in your body. It's all connected. It's ultimately a matter of how to manage your body and mind. You cannot win the game of life by focusing only on one and ignoring the other. They go hand in hand. Learning how to manage the body and mind is the key to living a happy and peaceful life.

Example #10: Keita's Story
There was a man named Keita who had been depressed for over 13 years when he first came to my workshop. He had a high-pressure situation early in his career that he didn't handle well and he subsequently fell into a deep depression. He came to my workshop and had a revelation. At the end of three days he left elated. He then returned for my next workshop, and the first day he looked more like a zombie again. He was

completely depleted. The workshop empowered him and he left feeling great. This happened a few times.

At the next workshop, he again looked stressed so I asked him what was going on. He explained that he worked for a big company and made a good living, but the company was "silently" showing him the way out. The labor law in Japan makes it difficult to fire people, so companies put employees under extreme pressure by yelling at and verbally abusing them. I sensed that the Universe knew that wasn't the place for him to shine so I told him that he might want to start actively looking for a new opportunity. He said, "No, I have a family and even though my working circumstances are not good, it still pays me well. I must stay. I can't just quit."

Two months later, he told me that he had been fired. Because he was not prepared, it hit him hard. He was on the verge of suicide. Once again, he signed up for my workshop, but two days prior he said, "I might not make it." He wanted to end his life. He was overmedicated, taking sleeping pills as well as anti-depressants, and did not appear to be himself. I told him that if people come to my workshop without medication, I can help them because words can heal. When people are over-medicated, words do not reach their soul. I told him it would be a tough decision, but if he could go without his medication and come to my workshop, I would do my best to help him. He said it was very hard but he made it to the workshop, and by the end of the three-day workshop, his depression lifted permanently.

Keita always loved being in nature so he now works doing guided hiking tours. Being in nature makes both his body and mind feel peaceful, which allows him to shine.

(Disclaimer: Do not stop taking your medication because of what you just read. Consult your doctor first.)

So, as you can see, when one door closes, another door opens. We just need to be open to the fact that there is always a way out. Once we open not only our eyes, but also our hearts and minds, all things are possible.

Chapter Eleven

The Reward

The reward of doing everything that I've just talked about is the knowledge that you're on the right path. A lot of people ask, "What am I here for? What is my life purpose?" "How do I make the best decisions for my life?" "How can I make a difference in the world?" When you are doing the job that you know you are here for and it is what you are passionate about, that's the greatest feeling there is. It's not about money or social status. It's about the feeling you get when you are on your path. By connecting to your Life GPS and following that path and by living the life you believe is right for you, you will be happy. When you do what your soul is seeking, you become happy on a soul level.

When you are happy because you bought an ice cream, let's call that Level 1 happiness. When you do something that you've been searching for throughout your life, you are contributing, and you're rewarded for your contribution, maybe it's Level 4 happiness. Once you get to Level 4, you may be ready to forego a Level 1 pleasure or happiness. Instead of spending your time at the ice cream shop, you may choose to write or shoot a video so that you can convey your message to the whole world in the hopes of making a real difference. I am not saying it has to be one way or another, but it often is.

If you do everything presented in this book, you can be the master of your mind and your body, and therefore your life. You can be sure of what you are doing every second. That's true happiness on the soul level and proof that you are on your soul's path. Every person is here to be happy, but not many people take the time or spend the energy to be happy on a deeper level. By following these simple steps you will be closer to real happiness on the soul level and be on your soul's path. Once you know that, once you experience that, you can't go back to being lost.

Your Life's Mission

You are here to be happy. I haven't encountered anybody who doesn't seek happiness. However, not a lot of people think seriously about being truly happy. Many people settle for mediocre happiness, but that can change once you make a decision to be happy. It's about commitment to happiness. Once you make that decision, once you commit yourself to true happiness and nothing less, you then discover a variety of ways to be happy. Once you learn how to communicate with your inner self and are able to receive guidance in a critical moment, it is almost impossible to be lost in your life.

A lot of people come to me and say, "I'm completely lost in my life. What should I do?" The feeling of being lost is painful. I tell them, once you learn how to connect with your inner self and are able to receive guidance from within, it is impossible to be lost in your life. In fact, not only you are not lost, you become crystal clear about what's happening and where you are in your life. You know exactly why things are happening to you. You may believe by now that things do not happen by chance. When big things happen to you, there are always reasons behind it. Typically the purpose is your spiritual growth. The only question you need to ask yourself is, "In what way am I going to grow spiritually from this experience?"

I know that those experiences are sometimes painful. They are painful only because they are new experiences so you don't know how to deal with them. That's where the growth occurs. When it is easy to handle the situation, there is no growth. When there are no challenges happening in your life, you are not really growing. Whenever challenging situations occur, it's a great opportunity for growth. Through the process, new opportunities show up and new paths are shown to you. Everybody comes to crossroads in life. Life is designed that way. How would you feel about making the right decision at every juncture in your life? The lessons in this book enable you to make good decisions in every critical moment.

The biggest benefit of applying the lessons in this book is that you will choose a path in which you prosper. When you choose a path that is not meant for you, you do not prosper. Listening to your Life GPS will prevent that.

For instance, let's say there is something you would like to do on your soul level, but your conscious mind is afraid. So you decide not to give it a try and instead stay exactly where you are, taking no action at all. This is what I call a "bad decision" for your soul's path. When the universe sends you a clear message to change lanes and you don't, it can be brutal. The universe, however, does not take action to be cruel. Instead, when you experience roadblocks, it's guidance from the universe telling you to get out of that lane. When you resist the guidance from the universe, your path becomes harder and harder. If the environment is your workplace, you may feel like you are a candle in the wind. If it is a relationship, you will probably experience more stress than pleasure. If you continue to hold on to it, you could be dumped. If the guidance from the universe is to leave your residence and move to a new place, you might be kicked out by your landlord or your house could catch on fire.

I'm not saying this to scare you. What I'm saying is that the universe will find a way to kick your ass, if I may use that expression, to get you to take action. The universe does whatever it takes to nudge you in the right direction. When you do not listen to your soul's navigation system and take action accordingly, then "horrible" things may happen to you. Still, they are not disasters. They are simply strong messages from the universe to change lanes or to change environments. By understanding how life works, how the universe sends you messages, and how to find the open door in your life, you can avoid many troubles.

You don't have to go through as many tough experiences if you change lanes when you receive the first subtle message from the universe. I suggest that if something bad happens to you in the future and you feel lost or don't know what to do, come back to this book. Open a page randomly and find a message that resonates with you. Then act on it. No matter what information you receive or knowledge you gain, unless you act on it, your life is not going to change. This book is dedicated to helping you find the open door in your life, but it is up to you to walk through it.

Chapter Twelve

Next Steps

A lot of people live their lives on an emotional rollercoaster. Something happens, you react. When something good happens, you become happy and your mind and spirit goes up. When something bad happens, your spirit and vibration goes down. Your emotions go up and down so frequently that by the end of the day you're spent. By the end of the week, you're exhausted. By the end of the month, you feel like a zombie. There is a way to prevent this from happening. This book offers an alternative. I suggest that you read this book cover to cover to get the concepts. I recommend, however, not just reading it once but again and again until the messages become ingrained.

Whenever you feel like you are not the best version of yourself, pick up this book and connect to your inner self. Open the book at any place. Just follow your instinct. The page to which you open is the page where you can find the information you've been looking for. I've tried it many times and it works. I've seen other people do it as well. Or just simply look at the table of contents and see which chapter resonates most with you. Sometimes just one sentence, one phrase, or one paragraph can save your day.

If you find information that is applicable to your life in this book, don't ignore it. You have a resource to come back to. This book can stay with you for the rest of your life or until you master each concept. You can begin a new chapter of your life with this book. Also, I'm sure you are familiar with some of the concepts in this book, but when you end up reading about the same concept over and over in life, it's often because you have not yet mastered it. Hearing it is one thing; mastering it and applying it to your life is another.

Get Yourself Centered

Practice Zen daily and learn how to rest your mind whenever you want. When you first wake up in the morning, don't immediately go into "work mode." Don't cloud your day by opening emails or watching the news. Don't let these negative energies invade your space. Nobody wants to start the day with a stormy, emotional mind. Instead, meditate for ten to fifteen minutes. When you know that you are a soul and you take the time to connect with your inner self at the start of each day, then everything that happens can be viewed as nothing but information.

In Japan, there is a saying that goes, "Once you go out into the business world, you have to fight with seven samurais." What does that mean? When you are in business, sometimes the work environment can be against you. There might be people that try to jeopardize your work, sometimes even your boss. It can also apply to a non-business environment. Even in your community there may be people who attack you or call you names behind your back. Anything can happen but if your mind is clear, you can react more adeptly. So it's best to prepare your mind before something challenging gets to it. That preparation can make a big difference in your day. It is a great way to control your mind instead of letting other people or the environment control it.

Practice these Skills

In order to have your future align with the work you are doing in the present, it requires constant conditioning. As I mentioned earlier, when you go to the gym and exercise for two hours, you don't say, "I am done with fitness for the rest of my life." It takes a lot of repetition to master new skills and change old patterns. Most people have their belief system instilled in their childhood so depending on how old you are, you may have lived with your belief system for many decades. There is no need to let go of all of your beliefs. You only need to evaluate them and release or replace the ones that don't serve you. This process takes time and it's easy to fall back to your old belief systems initially because you lived with them for a long time.

If you feel deep down that an idea or concept I introduced in this book may serve you, familiarize yourself with it. Expose yourself to that concept as often as you can. Data shows that when you are exposed to something new, it's a good idea to focus on it and try to have it present in your system for three straight weeks. When you live with a new concept for three weeks, it becomes a part of you. That's one relatively quick technique to condition your mind in a new way. Don't be frustrated if you feel like you learned something and didn't immediately apply it but rather made a decision based on your previous belief system. It's a long process and takes repeated conditioning. It is almost as if you need to practice until you reach a level of spiritual fitness in your mind.

It is often said that the people who surround you determine your value. It's challenging to evolve when you hang out with people who have strong attachments to the conventional belief system that you are trying to release. Who you surround yourself with has a big influence on your thoughts, beliefs, and vibrations. When you are trying to transform to the next level, it's critical to surround yourself with people who live in the vibration in which you would like to be.

Let's say you are on level three right now and you'd like to go to level four. Find people who already live in level four and spend as much time as possible with those people. It is also important not to look down on your friends in level three, as yesterday you were there with them. It may sound like you are dumping your old friends, but in fact you may be helping them by showing them that transformation is possible by changing your thoughts, beliefs, and vibrations. By seeing your transformation, your old friends in level three may be the next to join you in level four.

There are many ways to keep yourself informed and aware while staying tuned to this spiritual path of learning. One easy way is to subscribe to a newsletter from an author you like. I recommend selecting a newsletter that enhances your mind and soul so it can work like a spiritual growth pacemaker for your life.

Going to a seminar or workshop is another great way to learn and also to find others who think similarly to you. Those who come to a seminar are often people who are ready to move up to the next level. Those are people who have made a decision to be out of their comfort zone and learn something new.

When you learn a new concept and share perspectives with others who also recently learned that concept, it's a great way to keep learning. You can learn a lot from watching videos at home; however, going to a live seminar and physically being in a place surrounded by other people's energy, including the speaker's, gives you a whole new experience. It also provides the opportunity to make new connections, form new networks, and enjoy a new learning environment.

Conclusion

I thank you for taking the time to better your life. By following the steps in this book, you will find your heart lighter, your head clearer, and your soul happier. Just remember that no matter what happens in your life, you are not a failure; you just need to find your next open door.

If you enjoyed what you read in this book and you would like to continue your spiritual journey with me, please feel free to sign up for my newsletter at **www.kaziso.com.**

It's a weekly newsletter in which I share different perspectives so that people can look at their situations from different angles. When people understand the messages and apply them to their lives, they choose different paths and become happier.

About the Author

Kaz Iso is one of the most respected spiritual leaders in Japan. His teachings have transformed the lives of millions in Japan and now he is bringing his teachings to the Western world.

His teachings have a great balance of spirituality and practicality. Based on his own rich life experiences, Kaz helps others connect with their higher selves to find guidance, clarity, and answers to any of life's challenges.

He is an international spiritual life master who wants to share his mission of hope and transformation with you. He brings together Zen philosophy and higher self-awareness, melding them with powerful business perspectives and personal strategies to fully awaken your mind, heart, and soul.

To learn how Kaz can help you when one door closes, visit him at

www.kaziso.com

or his official Facebook page at

www.facebook.com/kaziso333